D1808187

A PORTRAIT OF
WINDSOR

MARK STENNING

HALSGROVE

First published in Great Britain in 2007

Copyright words and photographs © Mark Stenning 2007

All rights reserved. No part of this publication may be reproduced, stored in a retrieval system, or transmitted in any form or by any means without the prior permission of the copyright holder.

British Library Cataloguing-in-Publication Data
A CIP record for this title is available from the British Library

ISBN 978 1 84114 541 9

HALSGROVE
Halsgrove House
Ryelands Farm Estate, Bagley Road,
Rockwell Green, Wellington TA21 9PZ
email: sales@halsgrove.com
website: www.halsgrove.com

Printed and bound by D'Auria Industrie Grafiche, Italy

INTRODUCTION

One of the best known and least known of Britain's historic towns, Windsor remains something of an enigma for tourists and inhabitants alike.

The continuous flow of tourists expands into a great flood from Easter until the end of the summer. Most of these are day visitors coming via one of the two railway stations or by tour coaches. They have been drawn by the chance to see inside the largest occupied castle in the world and even at second hand to have a sense of what it might be like to be 'royal.' Windsor is for them part of the heritage trail and their goal is the absorption of a little romantic history.

Those of us who have Windsor for our home are sharply conscious of change rather than stability; of the influence of the modern world rather than the dominance of the past. Throughout the twentieth century, by a relentless progression, the once small and relatively sleepy town of New Windsor became today's busy provider of food, drink and souvenirs that are essential to a tourist-based local economy.

But whilst from mid morning until late afternoon the visitors circulate around the centre of the town they rarely explore its fringes. Even in high summer the expanse of the Great Park is relatively free of tourists when you might suppose a little stroll down the Long Walk might come as a welcome distraction from jostling in queues or following the Castle's excellent audio tour.

'Windsorians' have somewhat retreated to the margins and have become more conscious of what remains of the town's Victorian expansion, seeing it as their private heritage. Commuters who occupy the new perimeter apartments look for ease of access to the railway stations or the motorway but the established residents enjoy the many hidden and surprisingly attractive corners of the town and riverside which they have made their 'secret garden'.

Mark Stenning is an ideal photographer to capture the many faces of the township that was created by the arrival of William the Conqueror's fortress in the eleventh century and that today still finds its existence dominated by the world-famous outline of the Castle. He has a creative eye that seizes the moment conveying a sense of 'what it might have been like to be there'. But he also has a love of detail making the observer 'stand and stare' at something that familiarity might have encouraged us to overlook. He enjoys the irony in the fact that the heritage-seeking tourist brings constant changes to the town. But he also values that which has been effectively preserved through friendly neglect, in the way you might find an ancient aunt's well used arm chair was actually made by Chippendale!

Canon John A. White LVO
August 2006

I would like to dedicate this book to Ali, Charley, and Mims

The Castle appearing on the skyline above The Queen Mother Reservoir.

A local game of cricket under the shadow of the Round Tower.

Wintery sunrise over the Thames.

Early in the morning the Castle is a peaceful place
waiting for the first tourists to arrive.

Above and opposite: Queen Victoria, who for the many years of her widowhood had
Windsor Castle as her home still makes her presence felt.

Underneath the steep Victorian tiled roof of the Curfew Tower the picturesque clock and its housing are preserved. From this tower the chapel bells ring out.

Opposite: The size of the flag or the Royal Standard depends upon the importance of the day and the strength of the wind.

The Henry VIII Gate remains the main entrance for those who live and work in the Castle.

A refurbished lamp at the entrance to the Henry VIII Gate.

The guardsman in Lower Ward having
some peace and quiet before
the tourists arrive.

The Queen's Windsor horses are still stabled in parts of the Victorian mews buildings.

Opposite: There has been a Castle in New Windsor since the days of William the Conqueror. Although it has been restored frequently the Castle preserves much of its medieval outline.

Even at night the presence of the Castle still dominates the town.

Security remains a central concern for the Castle as these elegant rising bollards demonstrate.

King Charles II laid out the Long Walk to serve as a piece of dramatic landscaping leading up to the Castle.

Until the eighteenth century the Long Walk came to an end at this point.

Overleaf: The Castle guards the railway viaduct that links Windsor to nearby Slough.

The Castle seen from the north east, always a favourite view for artists.

Dorney Common retains its ancient rural aspect despite intrusive signs of change all around.

In autumn mists the Castle's familiar silhouette appears especially romantic.

Windsor's response to the London eye? No, merely a new summer feature along the riverside.

Evening silhouette, the new and the old.

View of Wardroyal with its aerial walkways. The large area of terraced housing demolished to make way for this new development was used as a backdrop in such 1960s' films as 'Carry on…' and 'On the Beat' with Norman Wisdom.

Wardroyal won many awards in the sixties for its forward thinking architecture. Expectations were high that these would become 'dream homes'. However the dream never materialised and the development has come under much criticism over the years.

More like a royal palace than a public hospital, Windsor's Edward VII Hospital still serves the community.

At the base of the statue the four Guardians with their shields represent
Responsibility, Happiness, Wisdom, Kindness. Four principles
that any good hospital should have.

A new building in the running to become a part of Windsor's heritage.

Period property on the Windsor side of Eton Bridge put to new use as restaurants, shops and offices.

Still owner-occupied this distinguished house in Sheet Street is merely one room in thickness.

Sir Christopher Wren House built and designed by him for his family in 1676. Windsor was perhaps
a natural place for Wren to settle down in as his father had been the Dean of Windsor.

The Castle Hotel is a fine old Georgian Hotel providing one of the best views of the changing of the guard.

Opposite: Cayley's department store, once a Windsor landmark, photographed only weeks before it closed for business.

The balconies of the 'Star and Garter' provide ideal places to view great occasions.

Opposite: At the bottom of St Leonard's Road the old town fire-station has been converted into a vibrant arts centre.

Windsor's Theatre Royal nestles between shops,
restaurants and offices in Lower Thames Street.

Windsor's Theatre Royal had a chequered history until John Counsell reopened it for live theatre productions.

Windsor's Riverside Station links the town directly to London's Waterloo. The large doors piercing the long brick wall were made to allow the easy transportation of horses for ceremonial occasions.

Opposite: Christopher Wren's adventurous architecture for the Guildhall provided a room for the marriage of the Prince of Wales and Mrs Camilla Parker Bowles in 2005.

Above: Civic elegance in Windsor's historic Guildhall.

Right: Inside the Guildhall a close up of one of the four pillars of Portland stone which serve no purpose in supporting the floor above. The council were concerned about the unsupported floor and insisted Wren should put some additional support. Wren said there was no need and to prove a point the pillars do not touch the ceiling

The Prince Consort Cottages, a haven of peace and tranquility within Windsor.

Understated elegance and one of the most desirable roads to live in in Windsor.

Opposite: A quiet afternoon playing bowls.

The brand new Visitors Centre at Saville Gardens. The structure sits comfortably in its surroundings.

Saville Gardens Visitors Centre from the garden side.

The Valley Gardens near Saville Gardens and Virginia Water house the
National Rhododendron Collection and Heather Collection.

Opposite: Orignally known as the Bog Garden, but renamed Saville Gardens
after Eric Saville, Deputy Ranger who started it in 1932 with the
support of King George V. It covers an area of 35 acres.

Afternoon out for the family along the riverside.

Windsor Great Park – The Totem Pole was a gift from the Canadian people to HM The Queen in 1958. It is carved from a single log of Western Red Cedar and Weighs 27,000 pounds. It stands 100 ft. high and marks the Centenary of British Columbia (1 ft per year).

Local people can still take a peaceful stroll down
the Long Walk in the early morning.

Queen Elizabeth II, a lifelong horsewoman is celebrated appropriately by an equestrian statue in the Great Park close to where she rides regularly.

Opposite: A horse that seems to know the significance of its rider.
The equestrian statue of Queen Elizabeth II, in the Great Park.

King George III made Windsor his home and enhanced the Castle, its chapel and the surrounding park.
His equestrian statue dominates the skyline at the end of the Long Walk.

This roman imperial effigy of the most English of Hanoverian monarchs may seem somewhat incongruous.

Queen Anne's Ride. Stone commemorating a 1000 years of the office of the High Sheriff.

Linking the Castle with its chief occupant.

Plaque on wall.

Opposite: Enclosing the shortest street in England,
The Crooked House always gains the attention of visitors.

Sunday morning life in Peascod Street.

Before the shops open. Peascod Street looking towards the Castle.

The raising of the Royal Standard announces to Windsor and the world that the Queen is at home.

The visitor will find plenty to occupy the time in a trip to Windsor.

Bandsman of the Blues and Royals concentrates on his music as the band marches to the Castle for guard change.

The band of the Coldstream Guards returns to barracks along Upper Thames Street after the changing of the Castle guard.

A serving soldier proud of his regiment's distinguished history stands outside the Victoria Barracks.

An original Tudor house with associated shops in Peascod Street.

Windsor has a continental atmosphere
when the sun shines.

A popular place to eat and drink at the entrance to the Long Walk.

Old and new combined in Sheet Street make for a severe elegance.

The town, like the Castle, is the product of many different periods and styles of building as these rooftops demonstrate.

Many tourists find a horse and carriage a more suitable way to see Windsor than the tourist bus.

A few evocative remnants of the old town survive
in the narrow streets across the road from the
Henry VIII Gate to the Castle.

Thames Street with its collection of ancient and modern properties climbs the hill towards the Castle entrance.

Raise your eyes above the shop fronts and the secret of the antiquity of some of the High Street buildings is revealed.

The end of the line at Windsor and Eton Riverside Station.

The Windsor Central Station complex.

Opposite: A new use for an old station, Windsor's latest shopping precinct.

With only one active platform remaining the Windsor and Eton Central Station has become a centre for local nightlife.

Nightime in the Windsor Central Station shopping complex.

The Station complex looking towards the Castle.

Windsor Central Station can seem remarkably
quiet between the arrival and departure
of tourists and commuters.

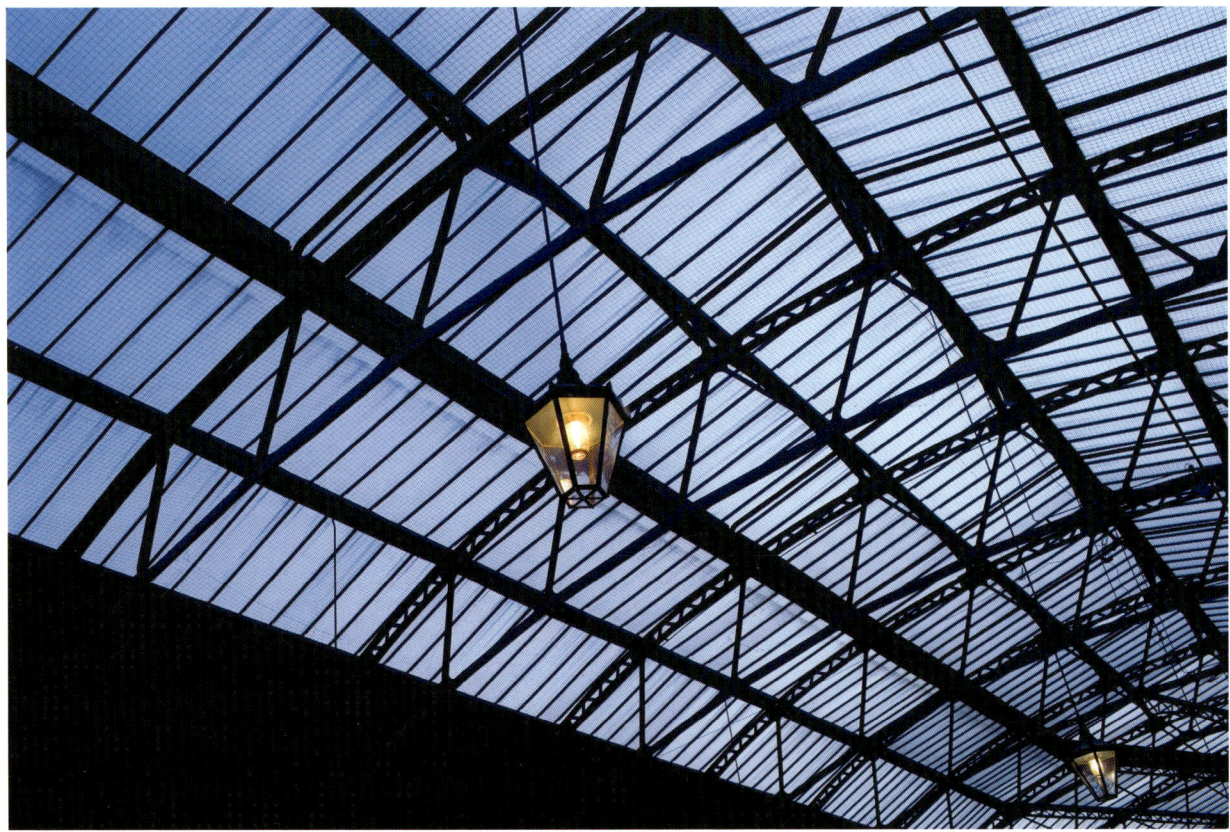

The vast glass roof that covers the station.

Victorian railing on the station platform.

Full scale replica of the GWR Archilles-class locomotive 4-2-2 measuring 57 ft long.
Originally named 'Emlyn' but renamed 'The Queen' to pull the six carriages of the Royal Train.

Alternative transport for the younger traveller.

Corner of Windsor Central Station.

Opposite: St John's Church in the High Street serves as a venue for concerts and events, especially during the annual Windsor Festival.

Weather vane – St George slaying the Dragon on top of
St George's School, Windsor.

Opposite: Travers' College, once the home of the ill-fated
Naval Knights is now the heart of St George's Choir School.
The school has its origins in the fourteenth century.

The first sight of the fifteenth-century St George's Chapel that greets a visitor when looking through the Henry VIII Gate into the Castle.

The West Front of St George's Chapel is a triumph of the English perpendicular style of architecture.

By kind permission of the Dean and Canons of Windsor

Looking much as it has done since it was built in the 1480s the Choir of St George's Chapel remains the centre for the daily worship of the College of St George.

By kind permission of the Dean and Canons of Windsor

King Henry VIII and the beheaded King Charles I share the same tomb beneath
the seventeenth-century pavement of the Choir.

Through the great West Door, beneath a wall of medieval coloured glass, come royal brides and the solemn processions of royal funerals.

By kind permission of the Dean and Canons of Windsor

By kind permission of the Dean and Canons of Windsor

Beneath the great columns of the perpendicular nave arcades, the altar appears diminished in size.

By kind permission of the Dean and Canons of Windsor

The view that Queen Victoria had when she crossed the walkway on the lead roof from the Deanery to the Royal Pew above the High Altar in St George's Chapel.

By kind permission of the Dean and Canons of Windsor

Above left: The St George fountain was added to the garth in the Dean's Cloister to celebrate the 650th anniversary of the foundation of the College of St George.

Above right: Modelled on a fifteenth-century wood carving from the Chapel, this vigorous St George completes the fountain in the Dean's Cloister.

Horseshoe Cloister was completed in 1480 by King Edward
IV and was used as lodgings for the Lay Clerks or
choirmen. Today it still serves this purpose.

Thomas Hardy designed All Saints' Church as Windsor's population increased.

A place where great trees from little acorns grow. Eton College Chapel in midday sunshine.

Looking from the Castle across the Thames to Eton and Slough.

Remains of the Day – football in Eton.

The Brocas Fair has been visiting Windsor
and Eton for over a century.

Once a sleepy town alongside the famous Eton College, Eton is now creating a new identity for itself.

Opposite: A good investment! This early post box will still take your letters!

The Eton Rowing Lake waits patiently for the 2012 Olympics.

Quads on the Eton Boating Lake.

The Queen reopened a restored Eton Bridge in her Jubilee year 2002. It is now a traffic-free pedestrian zone.

One of Eton's best known restaurants has the advantage of views of the Castle and the river from the dining room.

Opposite: A subtle play of light and shade on Eton Bridge.

Elegant restaurants and luxury apartments now
line the Thames across Eton Bridge.

A pancake race over Eton Bridge sponsored by a local coffee shop.

Opposite: Royal swans on the Thames.

It is difficult to lose the Round Tower even up river.

Windsor provides ideal moorings for Thames' pleasure crafts.

Once the Thames was Windsor's main traffic artery. Now it adds to the distinctive beauty of the town and its surroundings.

The setting sun colours the Windsor landscape.